Tea Attitudes

Tea Attitudes

A Blend of Tea, Life & Faith

Devotions to Warm Your Spiritual Heart

PAMELA G. KENNEDY

Hardcover ISBN: 979-8-3726142-1-5

Paperback ISBN: 979-8-3859722-4-1

First Edition, 2023

Printed in the United States of America on acid-free paper.

Cover and book design: Patricia Bacall Garver, bacallcreative.com

Dedication

To my parents, for their unconditional love and support throughout my life.

To my children, for their helpful advice and creativity in order to maintain a current and relevant perspective.

To my husband, for all of the above, as well as his patience and encouragement that have enabled me to achieve dreams and goals I would not have thought possible.

Contents

Introduction

The tradition of afternoon tea began in the 1800s by the Duchess of Bedford. She desired a snack before the customary late dinners of that time, and her inclination eventually became a regular social event with her friends. I was introduced to this experience over twenty years ago, and it has become a tradition in our family too. Over the years, there have been several moments from our tea dates that stood out to me in particular as having underlying life lessons. Some of these are presented in this book. All of the stories here are drawn from my memory and impressions from actual tearooms. I have purposely not named the establishments because I am not critiquing the restaurant and do not presume to be an expert in culinary arts.

One of my favorite Bible passages is from Jesus' Sermon on the Mount, the Beatitudes, found in Matthew 5:1–12. The words and rhythm are beautiful and inspiring. After some study, I view it not only as set of ethical guidelines, but also as a progression of Christian faith:

Blessed are the poor in spirit, for theirs is the kingdom of heaven.

Blessed are those who mourn, for they will be comforted.

Blessed are the meek, for they will inherit the earth.

Blessed are those who hunger and thirst for righteousness, for they will be filled.

Blessed are the merciful, for they will be shown mercy.

Blessed are the pure in heart, for they will see God.

Blessed are the peacemakers, for they will be called children of God.

Blessed are those who are persecuted because of righteousness, for theirs is the kingdom of heaven.

Similarly, the chapters of *Tea Attitudes* provide a progression:

Accept God's Grace

Forgive Your Past

Discover Unique You

Develop Inner Grace

Create Your Space

Define Your Choices

Grace with Confidence

Leap of Faith

This book is a testimony to my faith and beliefs. I have wanted to share these thoughts and memories for some time. Throughout these pages, I hope you will feel blessed and encouraged.

For it is by grace you have been saved, through faith—and this is not from yourselves, it is the gift of God.

Ephesians 2:8

As You Wish

Accept God's Grace

Cold and drizzly. I enjoy exploring even when the weather is brisk and damp, and this was a typical London winter's day. To visit and not experience the bluster would feel like the city was withholding one of her charms.

My destination this afternoon was a famed hotel tearoom. This grand hotel was set sedately off the busy thoroughfare, an impressive icon of luxury. The moment I entered, the *maître de* whisked my outer jacket away to a secure, hidden location. My footsteps floated on the padded carpet as the hostess escorted me to my reserved seat. This afternoon I was alone—and I relished every quiet moment.

Rising from the center of the room, a white latticed gazebo encased a polished black grand piano. My eyes were drawn upwards to the large, circular skylight directly above, fashioned from beautiful stained glass. I was in awe. The server, a petite young lady, gracefully approached and offered me the leather-bound menu as she welcomed me. She took my order and then asked, "Will there be anything else, *milady?*" *Milady.* I felt my jaw muscles faint, revealing an American infatuation with English peerage. With an inward panic I wondered, "Is she speaking to *me?*" I resisted

the urge to look behind me to see if she was addressing someone else and calmly replied, "No, thank you."

Raised in the Southern US, I am accustomed to hearing the occasional "ma'am." But *milady* made me feel special. This French term was appropriated by the English for addressing noblewomen. I am neither French nor English, and not of noble birth. Instead of protesting my lack of aristocracy, I appreciated the moment and thoroughly enjoyed the rest of the afternoon.

I reflected later how this undeserved respect was similar to the undeserved grace God has extended to us through Christ. Would I relish being termed a "child of God" as much as I perked up at being referred to as *milady?* On a less superficial level, that answer is yes.

Several years ago, I came to understand the difference between grace and mercy. Described in *Wilmington's Guide to the Bible,* "Mercy is the act of withholding deserved punishment, while grace is the act of endowing unmerited favor." We might be uncomfortable accepting things we know we do not deserve or titles we have not earned. Recall a time when you received a good grade or praise for a job well done knowing you did not earn it. Was it truly fulfilling? And yet, there is nothing we can do to earn God's favor.

Paul wrote in Romans 11:6, "And if by grace, then it cannot be based on works; if it were, grace would no longer be grace." From another perspective, if God—from the beginning of time—compelled us to love Him, that would not be love but a requirement. And so, if God's grace is obtained by works, then it is just a form of payment. God's grace is available to us either way, but it is through our love of God and belief in Jesus Christ that we can be assured eternal life.

In 1772, John Newton penned the lyrics for the hymn "Amazing Grace." This slave ship captain had rebelled against God most of his life, but through a series of events, he realized peace in God's unfailing grace.

Amazing grace, how sweet the sound
That saved a wretch like me.

Can any of us state with honest certainty that we have led a blameless life? Indeed, Paul describes our situation very simply: "For all have sinned and fall short of the glory of God." And when we compare our condition to God's holiness, it seems like a wretched comparison. That low point of humility and our awareness of the need for redemption initiate the beginning of our restoration. St. Augustine writes, "God pours his grace into empty hands." And from His overwhelming love for us, that grace fills our emptiness and spills over so that we might share it with others—much like the lyrics of Newton's song sung by so many souls throughout the years.

What are some of the unearned gifts you have received? The extra respect from my server during tea that day cost nothing, but it added immeasurably to my experience. Maybe you have experienced favor that has gone unnoticed. For example, someone who paused at the grocery checkout and allowed you to go ahead, or a

fee was reduced through kindness. Sometimes we are so busy looking ahead that we do not notice the people or circumstances that quietly help us on our way.

For the next week, I challenge you to recognize moments of helpfulness when your burden or stress was made even just a little easier. Wouldn't these be pleasant stories to share?

How about the grace you have shown to others? I believe we can show a little bit of grace every day. It flows out of our once-empty hands. We can pause before responding to an impolite cashier and offer a kind word instead. We can show appreciation instead of criticism. There are many opportunities to participate in church and community-based service. Service with grace means spending the gift of our time without considering the merits of the receiver. Catch the overflow and pass it on.

We had a family tradition for our children's thirteenth birthday. The birthday person had to perform thirteen small "trials" before they could open their gifts. A trial might include eating slices of raw vegetables or running around the perimeter of the house a certain number of times. It was a silly, lighthearted way to mark their transition into official teen years. Thank goodness we do not have to complete random tasks to be included in God's kingdom! He tells us that His grace is sufficient for all things. Grace is the bridge we cross to transition into His kingdom.

At the end of church services, Pastor would often give us the Old Testament blessing. The words of this blessing were given by God for the priests to pray over the Israelites.

"The Lord bless you and keep you. The Lord make his face shine on you and be gracious to you. The Lord turn his face toward you and give you peace." This prayer always makes me want to turn my face toward heaven and feel God's love, to look up and know undeserving grace. And in that moment, I feel worthy and noble in His eyes.

Reflections

Recall a moment when you felt an unexpected grace in your life. How did you respond?

Are there any current circumstances or opportunities for you to "pay it forward" and pass on God's grace?

Notes

If we confess our sins, he is faithful and just and will forgive us our sins and purify us from all unrighteousness.

1 John 1:9

Rearview Mirror

Forgive Your Past

Tea and friendship go perfectly together. Heading out to experience a new tearoom with a good friend and our daughters promised to be a memorable event, especially when our daughters are best friends as well! Conversation was in full swing as we parallel parked in historic downtown Roseville, a California city with deep historical roots from the 1849 Gold Rush. The beginnings of the Transcontinental Railway are also evidenced by the commemorative plaque at the restored train station.

We arrived at the address of a modest storefront and entered an unimpressive diner-style seating area. We cautiously informed the hostess we had reservations for afternoon tea. She brightened and promptly led us behind a heavy curtain at the rear of the main seating area. We found ourselves in a cozy, elegant room enveloped in mid-1800's décor. Gilt mirrors, velvet-patterned wallpaper, baskets of feather boas, and stands of wide-brimmed, fabulously decorated hats attended the space. We fully decorated ourselves with the props provided and placed our orders.

The first course, a beautiful stand of dessert pastries, arrived looking deliciously picture perfect. Moments later, a

lovely tray of scrumptious scones complete with clotted cream and jam. Then, when both of those courses were finished, a generous serving of various tea sandwiches. You've probably seen the slogan: "Life is short. Eat dessert first!" However, I did have the sensation of being Alice in Wonderland, where up is down and forward is backwards! Regardless of the order of service, it was a wonderful experience for us all.

On the drive home, I wondered, "What if our perspective of life was viewed in reverse, like the order of service today? What if, as we move forward through life, we periodically looked through our mind's rearview mirror?"

Starting with the present and heading backwards through time, imagine your memories as a road that began in your early life. A journey filled with exits and detours, sometimes beautiful and sometimes twisty. Thank goodness for the diversions that take us beyond the view from the shoulder of the road! They give us experiences from the simple paved path; they give us wisdom and depth. To be sure, many of these diversions bring us joy, satisfaction, and good memories, but why is it that we tend to dwell on wrecks we have left behind? God forgives our past, so shouldn't we let it go too?

When we are young, our parents direct most of our plans. They decide where we grow up, set expectations, and help guide our decisions. Gradually, as we get older we begin to mold our own ideas and accept control and responsibility for our decisions. Sometimes, our reasoning does not serve us well. We unintentionally end up on the side of the road with a flat tire or maybe a full head-on accident. Life moves forward and either way, we continue on down the highway of our life.

The nature of exits available during our life changes, maybe because of age, health, or finances, but also the lens through which we evaluate those choices is altered. How many of us look back and think, "If I had only known then what I know now…"? That statement is not fair to ourselves because our point of reference in that later moment has been shaped by all that has happened between those two points in time. I do not mean to include obviously poor choices, such as something illegal or inherently dangerous. If I had known that sandwiches would be served after dessert, would I have waited to have the sweets after? This seems like a trivial example, but the point is that because we do not know the future, we can only make decisions based on what we know in the present. Our parents made decisions for us while we were young based on their life experience, and our future choices will be shaped by events from our life. Paul encourages Christ's followers to "forget what is behind, and strive for what is ahead." That goal of striving ahead is the destiny and plan God has for you since before you were born.

What are the consequences of looking back? When we worry and dwell on regrets, we steal the precious moments of the present. We had a saying in our family to help us move past unpleasant situations after the conflict was resolved: "It's in the past now." It was a restart button that turned off the blame and moved forward with understanding.

In a less forgiving example, in the book of Genesis Lot and his wife were told to leave Sodom and Gomorrah before the cities were destroyed, and specifically to not look back. Lot's wife disobeyed and was turned into a pillar of salt. We do not even know her name. If we continually relive the negatives and that which should be destroyed, our lives will be little more than a pillar of salt. God calls us to live life abundantly and to enjoy the grace and forgiveness He offers.

A couple of years ago, my husband and I completed the Camino Frances, one of the routes for Camino de Santiago. The *Cruz de Ferro,* or Iron Cross, at about 4,900 feet is the highest point along this 500-mile journey. A Camino pilgrim tradition is to bring a rock from home that symbolizes a personal burden and place it at the foot of this cross. Before the trip, I struggled to find something meaningful and worthy enough to write on my rock for this spiritual place. Finally, just before we left, I noticed voices and feelings from my past wrecks flashing through my mind, and I made a commitment. Into that rock I would symbolically place all my past regrettable thoughts and words, then leave them at that cross. The flip side is that every time one of those uncomfortable thoughts would come to mind, I committed to change my attitude, words, and perspective in that moment and move on.

On that rock are the words: Forgiveness, Grace, Wisdom, Love, and Faith. I cannot go back and ask forgiveness for hurts or missteps I caused in my life, but I can treat people with grace, wisdom, and love in the here and now. The climb to the *Cruz* was arduous. I recited Bible verses and prayers all day just to make it to the summit. The cross itself is not ornate, but it is imposing in its simplicity. Leaving my simple rock at the cross was not a talisman or a wish for something good. It was a tangible memory for me to trust in forgiveness, and work to act with grace, wisdom, and love. It is with this faith that we can strive for the goals that we have been called to achieve.

Most of us can access directions to a desired destination, either through AAA or Google Maps. These maps show routes already built for us to follow, and even traffic patterns along the way. In a similar way, we need to create a guide within ourselves for our behavior and spiritual destinations. Proverbs 3:5 teaches: "Trust in the Lord with all your heart and lean not on your own understanding; in all your ways submit to him, and he will make your paths straight."

With all the beauty of this world and joy God desires for us, His straight path can be fulfilling and enjoyable, and there will be fewer collisions than the route we would choose on our own. Decide on your roadmap, set your course. And if dessert comes first…enjoy!

Reflections

Describe what you see in your rearview mirror.

Which decisions bring you joy? How could you symbolically place regretful choices in God's hands?

Notes

Yet, O Lord, you are our Father. We are the clay, you are the potter; we are all the work of your hand.

Isaiah 64:8

Pineapple Tidbits

Discover Unique You

Our family often recognizes important milestones by taking trips together, and invariably, one day will be set aside for ladies' afternoon tea. The occasion of my dad's sixty-fifth birthday brought us to the island of Maui, Hawaii, whose slogan is "Maui no ka oi," or "Maui is the best." It certainly holds a special place in the heart of our family! We have travelled there for birthdays, graduations, and our son and his wife even honeymooned there.

For this tea excursion, we arrived at a local resort restaurant in the early afternoon. As we approached the entrance walkway of this hotel, we were greeted by the beauty and perfume of plumeria and other fragrant tropical flowers. Polished marble floors and sturdy, dark wood columns graced the lobby. Following the clicking heels of our hostess, we were seated at a long wooden table set in an open breezeway. Magnificent sliding doors unveiled a full ocean view. Sounds from the nearby restaurant floated through the space as a large ceiling fan slowly moved the air over us. Natural light flooded the area and sunlight twinkled off the tops of the waves below. I felt my eyes could not open wide enough to absorb the breadth of the whole wonderful scene.

In addition to the fine selection of teas, we enjoyed tropical, house specialty drinks…the kind with umbrellas on top! We spent the afternoon sharing adventures and discoveries on the island. How nice to appreciate a common thread of island interest across our three generations. The service plates were beautifully prepared with many delicious selections. What impressed me was the way local flavors so effortlessly found their way into the menu. Whipped cream had a splash of coconut and bits of pineapple were blended into sandwich spreads. Unexpected and so appropriate! I have noticed other tearooms incorporating unique, local ingredients into their tea menus, such as an arboretum tearoom using edible flowers as decoration and flavoring. Embracing flavors and items distinct to different regions brings a sense of interest and appreciation to travel. In a similar way, it is important to celebrate the distinct gifts and qualities God has blessed and bestowed on us. Not only do our character traits influence our immediate community, but they enable us to fulfill God's special purpose for our lives.

How would you describe yourself? Take a few minutes, close your eyes, and think about what makes you unique. One hint: It is not just your fingerprints! At first, you may think, "I'm just like everyone else. I don't have any distinctive talents." Be patient and dig deeper. What qualities do you possess that you can always count on and that you bring to any situation? Recognize and appreciate them. Resist the temptation to define your traits by what you do, either for a living or out of habit. I would also suggest that whatever you discover in your thoughts is a package, like the tea experiences above. The beautiful view, ambiance of the restaurant, and the ingredients presented combined for a special and memorable event. Your temperament, experiences, tastes, and desires combine to express who you are. Flavors and textures blend to create something better and more interesting than the individual qualities alone.

Have you ever taken one of those online or magazine quizzes? In twenty questions, they are supposed to determine which TV personality you are most like, or even which fruit best represents you. On different days or moods, these conclusions about your personality will surely change. We take the quizzes because we are searching for an outside source to tell us who we are or what we are like. Shouldn't we want to be discovered by our inside self, through our connection with our Creator, respecting how God made us? David writes in Psalm 139:13, "For you created my inmost being; you knit me together in my mother's womb. I praise you because I am fearfully and wonderfully made; your works are wonderful; I know that full well." Respecting yourself acknowledges and praises God's work in creation.

When meeting a new group of people, one of the activities I do not enjoy is to "go around the room and tell us something about yourself." Because in the space of a few sentences, whatever small tidbits you choose to share will be what these people remember forever. That small bit of data does not define you and does not present an accurate package. Do you notice that you edit your response based on your perception of the group? I suggest that you are

really presenting what you think the group wants to hear, not who you really are or what you want to share. A better ice-breaker exercise might be, "What can we expect from you as we start our project?" or "What do you aspire to accomplish with our group?" This type of answer would allow you to share your core abilities and vision.

When my son was in high school, some students would tease him about a physical feature he had no control over. I loved his response: "Pick on something I can change." This exchange demonstrated that, though it was uncomfortable, he accepted himself the way he was created. This feature did not interfere with his character growth or determine the person he would become. As you review the qualities you defined above, how will you use and exercise those traits created in you to accomplish what you are called to do, even if you have an insecurity? Today, my son is a handsome young man, well-respected in his profession. He used the gifts and dreams he was given to accomplish significant goals and success.

In his book *The Purpose Driven Life,* Rick Warren discusses how God intentionally created us as individuals to serve him. Warren explains that we each have a unique SHAPE. Our shapes are formed by: <u>S</u>piritual Gifts, <u>H</u>eart, <u>A</u>bilities, <u>P</u>ersonality, and <u>E</u>xperience. Everyone has a distinctive shape and can therefore serve a world full of needs and differences. Because each of us is created for a unique ministry, there is no cause to compare or compete with others' work. In fact, it would be impossible. God alone sees our true motivations and efforts. We are called "to love the Lord your God and serve him with all your heart and with all your soul." It is the intrinsic qualities of your heart and soul that God wants you to express, and the blessings of your abilities and experiences that He desires you to employ during your lifetime.

I appreciate the distinct tastes, unique combinations, and varied presentations used by different teahouses. If you identify and grow your special abilities and share them with your community, these traits will align into the exceptional person you are destined to be. We are not meant to all be the same type or shape of individual. Encourage yourself to appreciate what makes you unique and give space for others to have the same freedom. Your qualities and gifts are the salt that gives flavor to this world. Paul writes to the Ephesians, "For we are God's handiwork, created in Christ Jesus to do good works, which God prepared in advance for us to do."

The table is set and there is a wide world of opportunity. Using your gifts for God's purpose is an act of gratitude and worship that will surely sparkle and reflect God's light in you.

Reflections

What character traits did you discover about yourself?

How could you find opportunities to use these gifts?

Notes

Finally, brothers and sisters, whatever is true, whatever is noble, whatever is right, whatever is pure, whatever is lovely, whatever is admirable—if anything is excellent or praiseworthy—think about such things.

Philippians 4:8

Potted Plants

Develop Inner Grace

The beauty of the Pacific Northwest coast is exceptional. Several years ago, my mom, daughter, and I set out on a driving adventure from Sacramento to British Columbia. Rugged cliffs and wild ocean views made for extraordinary scenic vistas. One of the highlights arranged for our eventual stay in Victoria was tea at one of the world's most famous hotels. As we exited a taxi on the corner in front of that imposing building, we were buffeted by a firm, brisk gust off the ocean.

We hurried up the steps inside and entered through heavy revolving doors. While showing us to our table, the hostess casually spoke of the impressive 100-year history of the tearoom and hotel. She related the royalty and celebrities who had graced the halls. All I can remember was the impression of tall, ornate columns, high coffered ceilings, and the floor-to-ceiling windows filling the room with light from the beautiful coastal scene outside. With a touch of elegance, large stands filled with full potted palms separated the space between customers. Our table was expertly dressed, and shortly after being seated, our menu choices were effortlessly received.

We were deep into enjoying our tea and conversation when suddenly, to our right, we heard a sudden woosh of greenery and clanging of metal as something thumped to the floor! The unexpected sound and confusion caused a wave of surprise throughout the hushed room. Our server had inadvertently backed into one of the ornate plant stands and sent it crashing straight in front of our table! With enviable poise, she excused herself and in mere moments, hotel support staff had whisked away any trace of the event. Accidents happen, but traces of this one did not last long. We have all felt sympathy for an employee who is having a bad day, and we hoped ours would not be unnerved. However, our server that afternoon exhibited a grace that blended seamlessly with the hotel.

An earlier chapter, "As You Wish," discussed the undeserved grace we receive from God and how we can express that in our own lives. This different inner grace exhibited by our server is that of the elegance of individuals who react and move with composure.

Recall a moment of anxiety that resolved well, or an individual you admire for their "grace under pressure." What characteristics of the person's behavior impressed you? For example, was it the tone of their voice or their organization of priorities? My three children attended a small Christian elementary school, and their third-grade teacher immediately comes to my mind. I observed this woman as a parent for three separate school years. At twenty or so students a year, that makes for approximately sixty children and over one hundred parents, just in the years my children were in her classroom. In those years, including field trips and regular class time, she served as an exemplary educator. She could correct a child's misbehavior while building their spirit, and diffuse a helicopter parent using demeanor and conversation that left no doubt who was in control of the classroom. And she managed all this with a smile and a twinkle in her eye!

At the time, I wanted to know what child psychology book she had read, thinking surely I would need to read it twice! Through my interaction with her, the source of her security and wisdom became evident. The gifts she exhibited did not come from any outside source, but from what she practiced from within. Jesus taught that "what comes out of your mouth comes from your heart." When your words and actions match what is in your heart, you are authentic. She connected with her students because kids have a keen sense to sniff out a fraud, and they believed in her. She was not only graced with the gift of teaching, but she was using that blessing for God's service.

In his book *My Heart—Christ's Home,* Robert Munger creates the metaphor of his heart as a house and walks Jesus through all the "rooms" of his heart. As the author tours his home, he views the contents through the eyes of a sinless Savior. He experiences discomfort from certain reading materials found in his living room that influence his thought, and realizes that faith is not fed by the same appetites found in this world. Neither is his workbench as productive as it could be for service. In the end, not only does the author realize God should have access to our

whole heart, but the way to truly change our lives is to submit that heart to Him. In this way, not only is Jesus our guest, but we "transfer title" to Him.

Are there items (behaviors, thoughts, or attitudes) in the small, dark corners of our heart-home we would be embarrassed to reveal or that are hard to admit? Once we go through Munger's exercise of identifying and cleaning out those rooms, we must decide how we will fill our hearts again, so that these less-than-perfect things will not be able to clutter and gather dust again. A verse in Galatians offers us a great start: "The fruit of the Spirit is love, joy, peace, forbearance, kindness, goodness, faithfulness, gentleness, and self-control." I encourage you to choose from these traits to refill your heart.

A wise adage states, "Our choices become habits and our habits become our character." My children's third-grade teacher practiced what was within. It doesn't work to just *think* we want our hearts to be a certain way. Just like an athlete or a professional speaker, we need to define our goals and core beliefs and practice habits to achieve those results.

In the many years of my Christian walk, I have been trying to improve the condition of my heart and mind. I realize true change starts from the inside. Bible passages such as, "Create in me a new heart and renew a steadfast spirit," "to be made new in the attitude of your minds," and "be transformed by the renewing of your mind" impress the importance of the origin of thought. One theme I am working on is to "infuse God's presence in your thoughts."

I made a long list of ways I might do this, but ultimately I came up with this simple prayer:

May my thoughts reflect your wisdom.
May my words reflect your grace.
May my actions reflect your love.
May my plans reflect your will.

I have printed this prayer on small cards and shared it with people who are important to me and people I have met on the Camino. What a blessing it would be to connect with each of these attributes of God and practice them in my life!

A few years ago, a great lesson was trending around the internet titled, "What's in your cup?" The premise is that we all carry around a cup containing the substance of our character—half full or half empty doesn't matter. At some point, we are going to trip or lose our balance. This disturbance could be a situation at work, in traffic, or maybe even at home. The contents of that cup we hold are going to splash out for the world to see. Like the plant stand falling to the floor of the restaurant and spilling from its container, there will be a mess on the floor. The challenge for us all is: "What would you rather clean up?" You see, how we choose to fill our cup really does matter.

Reflections

What do you find in the corner of your heart-home that has collected dust and influenced you for too long?

Will you decide to keep that space clean and empty, or will you fill it with something beautiful?

Notes

*If any of you lacks wisdom, you should ask God,
who gives generously to all without finding fault,
and it will be given to you.*

James 1:5

Drawing Room

Create Your Space

London's distinctive style of taxi cabs are black carriage cars reminiscent of the 1930s era. On this particular day, we waited impatiently outside our hotel for the familiar diesel engine rattle signaling the approach of one of these very London traditions. Our carriage driver was late. Knowing the delays caused by the city's heavy cross-town traffic elevated our anxiety about arriving on time for our afternoon reservation. This restaurant books out several weeks in advance, and with so few days at our disposal, we did not want to miss the opportunity to experience this highly recommended tearoom.

Harried as we were, we arrived somewhat on time and hurried to the entrance of the building. The doors opened and it was just like the comfortable feeling of shedding your shoes at the front door of your own home; our anxiety from the tense taxi ride slipped into a puddle outside that heavy-doored entrance. The fireplace surrounded by steadfast wood paneling warmed our senses. Booths and oversized, upholstered, barrel-back chairs invited us to relax and sit a while. The staff were efficient but warm.

Afternoon tea at this establishment is served in another English tradition, their Drawing Room. The term "drawing room" originated in the seventeenth century as the place ladies would "withdraw" to following a social dinner occasion. These early-era rooms were set aside to provide a relaxed area for more comfortable, intimate conversation. This restaurant's space drew us in and made us feel at home.

How do we create a home? The week before my wedding, my dad sent me a letter with his thoughts about what makes a house a home. Among these were a place to feel safe and a refuge from the outside world. I would include, it is a place where we surround ourselves with that which is dear to us. Some things might be sentimental, material items. For example, I have a set of cat figurines my husband bought for me when we were dating forty years ago. Some things are, of course, people. Even though I'm very satisfied that my children all have their own households, I hold their visits and company very dear. And some things are intangible, such as the family memories made in one house that cannot transfer to a new home, no matter how much they mean to me. Therefore, I am determined to create memories in our new home so they can fill the rooms and decorate the walls here, too. Home is a blend of the physical and sentimental aspects we love. And that is why it is so special and unique to each of us.

In a typical house emergency evacuation plan, the list of what to salvage includes important documents and photographs. If you had to recreate a home in a totally new location, what would you bring to connect the spirit of one house to the next? Or what would you use to develop an altogether new one? This might include tangible items, like my cat collection. But what about the intangibles, such as your values, habits, or sense of style? Just as we mentally plan for our career or define our life goals, intentionally creating a satisfying environment through nonphysical attributes is important, too. By identifying those intangibles that are significant, you can discard mental clutter that detracts from what you enjoy. Then you can work to enhance the qualities that already give you happiness, no matter where you are.

A family I know is building a new home. As the concrete forms were laid and rebar fitted, they asked their pastor to come and bless the proposed entryway. They wanted everyone who came through the front door to know God's blessing. Concrete and steel create the foundation of a house, but it is our values that support the foundation of our homes. *The Oxford Dictionary* defines values as "a person's principles or standards of behavior; one's judgment of what is important in life." These standards of what is important to you reflect in your home environment and on people who visit. They influence your family and the character they share with the world.

When couples marry, I Corinthians 13 is often read. It is a fitting blessing for the start of their lives together and the home they will create. Paul's last verse provides a summation of values for Christian life together: "And now these three remain: faith, hope and love. But the

greatest of these is love." Faith, hope, and love are like three strands woven together to form a cord not easily broken. The Drawing Room we encountered that day wove together the feelings of warmth, hospitality, and generosity, and the firm and friendly atmosphere dissolved all our stress at the door.

The importance of habits is not a new concept. In the sixth century BC, Lao Tzu wrote, "Watch your thoughts, they become your words; watch your words, they become your actions; watch your actions, they become your habits; watch your habits, they become your character; watch your character, it becomes your destiny." In more modern times, Stephen Covey authored the first of many versions of *The 7 Habits of Highly Effective People,* and even more recently, James Clear published *Atomic Habits.* Our routines provide a rhythm and structure to our homes and daily lives. Proverbs 31 describes the habits of a wife of noble character. To read through the list of activities and attributes of this woman can leave you exhausted or even feeling inadequate. Notice the last verse: "Charm is deceptive, and beauty is fleeting; but a woman who fears the Lord is to be praised." Respect and love for God are her motivation, and through this purpose she makes daily habits and choices that nurture her household and create a home.

Like a comfortable home, the arrangement of the Drawing Room enveloped us as we fell in from the outside. The placement of the furniture and the spaces prepared for us were designed for comfort and privacy. The décor incorporated special touches, such as intricate paneling and hushed curtains, that made it interesting. It portrayed a certain style. I admire and am intimidated by people who can style their homes. I have taken several online quizzes to find my style, and I am still confused. I cannot even pronounce *"feng shui"* correctly! A few months ago, I invited a decorator to help with some home improvements. He used the terms "public" versus "private" space. Innocently, I just thought of "front" versus "back" of the house. Defining the spaces his way made me realize I will show most of the public some things about myself, but I would have to know you pretty well before you would see the "back of the house."

How do we arrange and place not just household items, but also the personal values and experiences of our lives in our homes? "By wisdom a house is built, and through understanding it is established; through knowledge its rooms are filled with rare and beautiful treasures." The decorations of our homes are tangible expressions of what we want to share with our guests. But it is the experiences of understanding and intimacy with friends and family that truly make our home beautiful.

One of my favorite sayings is, "Walk with God in the garden of your heart." I enjoy the camaraderie of walking with friends, the gentle, unhurried time together. Imagine a garden that mirrors your values, habits, and style. Your yard space might show off beautiful, happy flowers, or maybe it provides nourishing fruits and veggies. A beautiful garden requires thoughtfulness, work, and preparation. A warm invitation into a beautiful place filled with intimate details is what I would want to present. My garden is

not perfect, but being on my knees pulling the weeds and preparing the rich soil to accept Christ's divine guidance, help, and renewal is the place to start.

The Drawing Room provided a place of refuge and warmth for us after an uneasy morning. As we prepare our homes and our hearts with important intangibles, we can explore and enjoy them all in abundance. And remember, there's a place to leave your muddy shoes just outside the door.

Reflections

When visiting with family and friends, what qualities make you feel welcome?

What values do you respect?

How could you blend these into your own lifestyle and home?

Notes

Notes

Therefore, everyone who hears these words of mine
and puts them into practice is like a wise man who built
his house on the rock.

Matthew 7:24

Serve Yourself

Define Your Choices

Expect the unexpected. On our way to afternoon tea, offered by an upscale, downtown tearoom, there was the anticipation of luxurious attendance: a gracious environment, impeccable service, and culinary excellence. After locating parking in the nearby, congested city block, we entered a prestigious Washington, DC hotel on this brisk early afternoon looking forward to a little indulgence. Greeted by a uniformed *maître de,* we obediently followed from the airy, bustling check-in area to a long, lonely corridor. The electrical cords lining the hallway did not deter our spirit. The passing construction worker did not arouse our suspicion. Even as our steps slapped across temporary cardboard flooring, we were confident our destination would be beautiful. As our guide directed us into the makeshift space, each of us experienced a clumsy moment of confusion. Then reality hit. The restaurant was under construction, and this wayward room was assigned to us.

My first impression as we entered the hotel's temporary tearoom was industrial and cold. Cafeteria tables and a stainless-steel buffet lay before us. A perfunctory server, who probably felt demoted, slipped into the room. The burring

of drills and clanging of pipes vibrated along the walls. Soon our composures realigned, and we determined to enjoy being together in unique circumstances. The surroundings faded throughout our conversation, and I began to appreciate the freedoms of our first-ever self-serve tea. The most immediate of these freedoms was that we were able to choose what we wanted from the buffet selection. This opportunity for self-direction actually brought on hesitancy and indecision. Approaching the shiny buffet, I realized the responsibility for making my own choices. How much to sample? Too much, and I would feel an uncomfortable waistband. Which ones? Unlucky choices, and I imagined the proverbial box of chocolates with wasted, half-eaten confections. I felt pressure trying to make the right choice.

Individuals approach choices with different perspectives and abilities. For some personalities, making decisions comes naturally, while for others the act seems daunting. How we make choices also varies and develops throughout our lives. As we mature past our mid-twenties, decision-making shifts from the more emotive area of the brain to the prefrontal cortex, considered to be the rational and analytical part of the brain. Another important aspect of decision-making is seeking spiritual counsel. Prayer provides an opportunity to listen to that still, small voice. Isaiah reminds us, "Your ears shall hear a word behind you, saying, 'This is the way, walk in it,' when you turn to the right or you turn to the left." Personality, physiology, and prayer influence our decision-making skills.

What are decision schematics that can help us? You may have heard the advice, "Make two columns and write out the pros and cons." A few years ago, my husband and I were making a big relocation decision, and not content with just two columns, we created a "decision matrix." Even then, two of the outcomes were tied! In 2014, Ruth Chang presented a TED Talk titled "Hard Choices." She discussed that often when we compare options analytically, they will seem "on par" and they can both be viable, healthy choices. To help evaluate between two even choices, she advises to look more closely at which one aligns with your values. What we choose should represent our core. Let's take this one step further and discuss how to define that core.

Stephen Covey, in his book *The 7 Habits of Highly Effective People,* presents an exercise to create your own personal constitution. The first step is to list all the things you would walk across a street for. Besides family and friends, mine might include chocolate or Starbucks. Next, imagine yourself at the top of a skyscraper on a windy day. There is a four-inch beam connecting to another tower. What would you cross that beam for? Your list just got a lot shorter! This is where you meet the heart of what is most important to you. His suggestion goes one step further, and I think it's powerful. Under each of those categories most dear to you, write two or three action items. These serve to propel you in a direction consistent with where you want to be. And those hard choices from earlier? Hopefully, this brings some clarity to those as well. A casual comment by our son, who had recently reached the ripe age of twenty-

five, turned on the light bulb for our relocation decision. He asked, "Why would you move across the country and retire to a town like the one you just left?" The basis of our move was for a new start and new experiences, and his comment was spot-on. Instead of setting up in parallel, we needed to expand into a different horizon. His outside perspective brought us back to one of the core expectations for our move.

When I approached the buffet that day, I paused, realizing that the implications of my choices were also my responsibility. I was expected to take action. What can motivate us past indecision? In his book *4000 Weeks,* Oliver Burkman discusses why people have a difficult time committing to decisions. Our mind can create an infinity of outcomes. As long as we have not made a definitive choice, all of those outcomes are still possible. But he argues that once we make a choice, it becomes all the more substantive and precious because of all the possibilities we give up for it, and we should relish that.

I believe if our values from the Covey exercise above include and prioritize that which is heavenly, the return is a blessing and pleasing to our soul. A verse in Psalms 37 states, "Take delight in the Lord, and he will give you the desires of your heart." Our simplest choices create an environment from which we build our lives. Aligning those steps with God's plan for us cannot help but guide us through even our most challenging decisions. If I replace the feeling of being overwhelmed with an attitude of gratefulness, it immediately puts this decision into perspective.

When thinking of examples of difficult decisions, I replay the moment in *Phantom of the Opera* when Phantom demands of Christine, "Make your choice!" She must choose between a life with him or Raoul's safety. Our real-life choices do not usually have such serious consequences. They can, however, have significant implications for our lives. After Moses' death, Joshua led the Israelites in their conquest of Canaan. Near the end of his life, he gathered all the leaders of the Israelite community to covenant again with God. Joshua reminded the nation of all the Lord had done for them since their exodus from Egypt. Twice, he challenged them to renounce all other gods from foreign lands. In this passage, he proclaimed, "Choose this day whom you will serve…But, for me and my household, we will serve the Lord." Joshua did not ask, rather he *demanded* that the Israelites focus singularly on serving God.

In his love for us, God has given us freedom of will, including the ability and responsibility of independent choices. Will the guidance you seek and the priorities you choose produce the results you value? I don't remember exactly what buffet choices I made that cold, wintry day, but I'm sure I went back for seconds!

Reflections

Recall a thoughtful choice from your past. Were you happy with the outcome?

What values helped guide you?

What did you learn from that process that you might use in the future?

Notes

*You will keep in perfect peace him whose mind is steadfast,
because he trusts in you.*

Isaiah 26:3

In the Corner

Grace with Confidence

For many years, my parents and I lived on opposite coasts, not seeing each other very often. When an opportunity came for me to accompany them on a business trip, I eagerly accepted. During the trip, we set aside time for a favorite pastime: afternoon tea. The tearoom we chose occupied the first floor of a boutique hotel on the corner of a busy city street, just across from a large public garden. The rush of city buses and diesel motor cars filled the space between the buildings as Mom and I exited a cab. A sense of escape enveloped us as we pushed open the single, main door.

Upon entering the well-kept brownstone, we immediately felt like we were passing into the library at a distinguished estate. The wood paneling on each wall held floor-to-ceiling bookcases, and the mullioned windows were framed with heavy curtains. Sofas and settees had been arranged to create intimate conversation spaces. The host showed us to a small table tucked into a window alcove sheltering us from the outside bustle. The atmosphere was hushed and comfortable. I remember appreciating the relaxed, friendly time with my mom.

After serving us champagne and our pots of tea, the tall, liveried waiter placed white porcelain bowls filled with full-sized strawberries and matching pitchers of cream in front of each of us. A look of confusion passed between Mom and me. Was the cream for the tea or the strawberries? Were we supposed to pour the cream into the berry bowl? Do you delicately cut the fruit whilst it is in the cream, or before? Our colonial American pride and desire to remain poised, not upsetting the balanced vibe of the room with possible sniggers, prevented us from asking the server what to do. It was a small moment, and we had a giggle over it later. What to do with a bowl of fruit is not, in itself, a big deal. However, I later thought about that small bit of awkwardness and wondered why social situations can cause unease.

There are many reasons why we may feel self-conscious in social situations. Adam and Eve were the first to introduce the concept of being underdressed. And in so doing, they invented awkwardness. Dr. David Braucher tells us in his article "Why Do I Feel So Awkward?" that this discomfort can arise from an unexpected conflict, an odd encounter, or even a new experience. Mom and I that day were sensitive that we were in a different country with different customs and were aware that we did not want to do anything socially curious that would attract attention. While it is normal to feel some anxiety in unfamiliar settings, Dr. Braucher encourages people to grow past those moments, because such experiences broaden their comfort base and prepare them for future situations. When approaching difficult moments, my quick prayer is often, "Heavenly courage and grace with confidence." A better solution that day would have been to put our pride aside and gracefully ask our server to explain the usual way for this course.

How we handle ourselves in uncomfortable situations can demonstrate aspects of our character. How do we portray grace with confidence? Some first steps are to be honest, not make excuses, and move past the moment. Of course, a sense of humor can go a long way to diffuse tension!

When our children were growing up, we had a saying: "If you're in a hole, quit digging." Every time you try to deflect or redirect, it's just one more shovel of dirt. Owning a situation demonstrates your confidence, and not lingering on the issue helps everyone press forward. Blogger Lucy Sixsmith writes that faith allows her to give all her awkwardness to Jesus, and that He can help her out of the hole, level the ground around the hole, or even use that hole for better things. Paul writes to the Romans, "God can use all things for the good of those who love him." Awkward moments can be useful for growing our faith and preparing us for the future. When we have a chance to practice our integrity, we are creating worthy habits.

If a plant is kept in the dark, how much will it grow? If a light is under a box, who will see it? Pastor John D. Barry, author of *Jesus' Economy*, asserts that God wants us to be in awkward situations for two reasons. The first is that they make us realize we don't know it all, and the second is because these moments are memorable. When we recognize that we don't have all the answers, it

encourages us to turn to God in prayer, asking the Holy Spirit to guide our behavior. The uniqueness of these experiences impresses them in our memory so that we actually learn from them. If all our days were ordinary and convenient, we would not consistently need guidance. Barry teaches about "Hard Prayer." This is not a genie-in-a-bottle prayer, but consistent, focused, and authentic prayer that develops a relationship with God. In Luke 11, Jesus teaches about the ability for the Holy Spirit to dwell within an individual indefinitely. This was a new concept for the Jewish community, because in the Old Testament, the Spirit would only come temporarily and to certain individuals. The primary reason for Jesus' ministry was to bridge the gap between humanity and God, and allow God to dwell in us. Uncomfortable situations keep us humble, and that humility is the entry to faith. A faith that is a light in the darkness can move mountains and even, in small ways, change the world.

As with my simple tea experience above, there are many opportunities to represent "grace with confidence" both for ourselves and others. A step toward this assurance is to evaluate our audience on the stage of life. For example, on past mission trips, I've found myself worrying about how the team perceived my efforts or if they misread the motivation behind my decisions. This made me insecure and hesitant to participate. The better mindset would be that my work and behavior should be guided by the Holy Spirit and done to glorify God. Only He can know my true heart. Sixsmith relates that her faith allows her to "abandon the habit of feeling embarrassed." Her term "habit" resonates with me, because it is a social pattern to check how others view us. Paul writes that because, in Jesus, we have a High Priest in heaven who has lived amongst us and knows us, "we can approach the throne of grace with confidence" and hope for mercy. Similarly, when we behold others with the same amount of grace God shows us, we can see beyond their awkwardness and insecurities. Then both our social lenses can fade away.

It takes courage to admit when we are wrong or don't know something, and it reveals confidence to continue moving forward and engaging in new experiences. We also need grace to free ourselves and others from those uncomfortable situations. How do we balance between overconfidence and subservient grace? Victoria Riollono, of victoryspeaks.org, phrases it nicely: "Carry the grace of a servant with confidence from the Lord." I regret not asking our waiter that day if there was a certain custom for what he served. The lesson of humility from that moment has opened subsequent dialogues for learning different options and new ideas. It has brought experiences that make my world a little larger, a little richer, and definitely less sheltered than that corner table.

Reflections

Reflect on a recent awkward situation you have seen or experienced. How did the individuals display grace or confidence?

Describe how someone could "carry the grace of a servant with the confidence of the Lord."

Notes

Now faith is being sure of what we hope for and certain of what we do not see.

Hebrews 11:1

At the End of the Hall

Leap of Faith

Fall is a pleasant time to visit Las Vegas. My mom, sister, and I all have birthdays during this time of year, and a trip to this iconic celebration destination was in order! Needing a break from the glitz of the Vegas Strip, we intentionally made our customary tea reservation away from the hype and hotel area. The listed address led us to a large, industrial warehouse that blended in with its dusty gray neighborhood. The various painted signs posted to the building advertised the businesses within, using tired names like "Grandma's Attic" or "Creations by Polly." Looking around to make sure we were at the correct place, we crunched our way inside from the gravel parking lot. We were struck with the sight of dozens of stalls that organized the vast interior and vendors who sold everything from antiques to homemade goods to used clothing. The height of the ceiling hushed the busy commerce below, and huge ceiling fans twirled lazily above. We had definitely left the land of tourists!

One end of the building was reserved for the snack bar area, which was where we found our tearoom. The simple, round tables were covered with pretty, vinyl-coated tablecloths and topped with vases holding a simple, fresh

daisy. The plastic outdoor chairs scraped noisily on the polished concrete as we found our seats. Two young women worked the restaurant. We could see one busy in the kitchen and the other serving tables, both wearing ponytails, smiles, and clean aprons. The homemade menus were nicely printed with basic but adequate choices for a tea luncheon. Not knowing what to expect, we placed our orders and settled into conversation about which booths we might want to visit afterward.

Our tea was served in pretty pots with delicate cups. The sandwich selection was unique and delicious, and the dessert pastries were created with care. I remember noting that subtle flavors had been added to the traditional spreads that created interesting and unique sandwiches. Afterwards, as we wandered through the maze of booths, I pondered how such a lovely tea experience could exist at the end of this steel-and-girder building. I recalled the concentration of the women as they worked their tasks and utilized their talents. I admired them for their efforts and hoped their location was a stepping stone to a more polished location in the future. It seemed to me they were reaching out and taking a chance to fulfill a dream. Some might call this a "leap of faith."

An earlier chapter in this book discusses the process of making choices. What is the difference between making a choice and taking a chance? A choice can be as simple as ordering chocolate or vanilla ice cream, or as complicated as purchasing a home. But a chance, now…that introduces the aspect of external factors you might not be able to control.

It holds the probability of even fewer known consequences than a choice, and it involves risk.

Let's consider three types of risk: physical, emotional, and financial.

Physical risk might include questions regarding health. For example, you might ask, "If I take this drug, will it cause cancer later?" or "Will this medicine cure my cancer now?" An emotional risk might involve relationships. Do you tell someone, "I love you," or decide to avoid entanglements? Assessing financial risks is a little more straightforward. Your bottom line will be either higher after you "gamble at the tables" or you "invest in the market." An individual who can count cards may actually have better odds in Sin City than if that same individual were to choose stocks from the supposedly more respectable market. With all of the above scenarios, the question is: What will you put your faith in, and how will outside events affect your outcomes?

Faith can be described many ways. At its basic form, faith is belief in something without empirical evidence. The ladies in the tea restaurant had enough confidence in their dreams to work their business without knowing the future. Taking a chance, as above, is having faith without knowing the external factors that might affect the choice. There are many examples of faith presented in the Bible, and throughout history, God used people who were willing to take risks. Abraham left his home in Ur on God's promise of a new land for him in Canaan, which was a faith journey of over one thousand miles. Through him, God created the nation of Israel.

There are other examples of people, such as Moses, who needed encouragement to meet their purpose. He was hesitant to confront Pharoah because of his speech impediment. Jeremiah writes that God "has plans to prosper you and not to harm you, plans to give you hope and a future." Therefore, we trust and have faith in His plans for our talents and abilities. Jesus' parable of the bags of gold encourages us to use the gifts and blessings He has given to us to the best of our ability in order to compound those gifts. Remember in the "Pineapple Tidbits" chapter the exercise to discover your unique qualities? What are some of the qualities and gifts that God has given to you that you can use to return to Him?

When I have time, baking is very relaxing and enjoyable for me. Several years ago, a woman moved into our neighborhood. In what seemed like a low-risk situation, my young daughter and I made her a welcome cake. Walking down the street toward her house, I thought about how the lady might enjoy our cake, the conversation we might have, and plans that might unfold in the future. I felt good about this teaching moment for modeling social graces to my daughter. When the new neighbor answered the door, we introduced ourselves and pointed to our house for reference. I clearly remember, she took our offering and blankly looked at us. She barely uttered, "Thanks," and then firmly shut the door. Apparently in this instance, my God-given talent was not to be shared!

Deflated as we walked home, I reflected whether my daughter would avoid reaching out to others after the unwelcome response from this "teachable moment." Many years later, that same girl took a chance at a new school and struck up a conversation with an upperclassman during high school gym class. They have since married and just celebrated their sixth anniversary. In both of these examples, we took an emotional risk and were simply reaching out for friendship. We couldn't know the eventual outcomes from either situation, but we stepped out in the faith of kindness.

Sometimes fulfilling a dream means taking a chance. Sometimes reaching for God's will means taking a risk. Like an acorn, unless we grow out of our shell, we will not reach toward the sky. There is a whole forest waiting for people to take their next step. Your dreams do not have to change the whole world or the course of history; they just need to strengthen the spark inside of you that adds dimension and fulfillment to your days and enriches the community around you. You may not lead a nation into a new land, like Abraham or Moses. But the gifts you share with others may enhance their day or influence their lives.

I do not know what became of the ladies in that Las Vegas tearoom. But I do know that, for that brief moment in time, they were following their dream and our experience in their enterprise was a memory I hold dear.

Reflections

Review your answers from previous chapters. Do you see a common theme?

Do you feel a spiritual nudge toward a new venture in your life? Or a confirmation for service you are already involved with?

Using your God-given gifts and talents, what might be a few next steps to begin or enhance your work for God's service in your community or within yourself?

Notes

Notes

Afterword

Family, friends, and food. These are important pieces of the memories I hold from my family's tradition of afternoon tea. A tradition that has served as a rite of passage for new in-laws and growing children, and as celebration for birthdays and other milestones. Jesus incorporated these elements into His ministry as well. His first miracle was turning water into wine at a wedding reception at the request of His mother. From another miracle and a lesson of faith, He instructed His disciples to feed over five thousand people from baskets with just a few fish and a couple of loaves of bread. As well, the Christian tradition of communion originates from a Passover seder the night before Jesus was crucified. In this instance, He merged traditional aspects of this Old Testament sacred meal into a rite of remembrance for the New Covenant He was creating for mankind.

Jesus presented The Sermon on the Mount early in His ministry in the area of Capernaum near the Sea of Galilee. For hundreds of years, the Jewish people were accustomed to living under the laws found in the Talmud, religious rules that were often interpreted very legalistically by their scholars and priests. Jesus' ministry was not to abolish these laws, but to bring their purpose back to the hearts of the people. That purpose was to place God at the center of their lives and to serve their fellow man through respect and grace.

The Beatitudes are an integral part of this Sermon that highlights our dependence on God and the grace in which we are called to live. In them, I view a progression of the Christian faith as follows:

Blessed are the poor in spirit.

We humbly recognize our need for repentance.

Blessed are those who mourn.

We regret our past and long for spiritual connection.

Blessed are the meek.

We approach God with a sincere and gentle spirit.

Blessed are those who hunger and thirst for righteousness.

We are eager to learn and practice God's ways.

Blessed are the merciful.

We can show understanding and love to others.

Blessed are the pure in heart.

We seek to behave with right intentions on God's path.

Blessed are the peacemakers.

We interact in our community to share God's love and promote reconciliation.

Blessed are the persecuted because of righteousness.

We can stand against opposition on God's strength.

The blessings of this right relationship with God are not focused on temporal, material things, but rather, to realize an inner joy and peace that cannot be removed or shaken. The chapters of *Tea Attitudes* also provide an outline for progression for Christian faith:

Accept God's Grace

God's grace is unearned.

Forgive Your Past

Forgiveness is available through faith in Jesus.

Discover Unique You

God has created you for a purpose.

Develop Inner Grace

Develop God's understanding in your heart.

Create Your Space

Design a God-centered lifestyle.

Define Your Choices

Seek God's wisdom as a foundation for action.

Grace with Confidence

Let God guide your behavior.

Leap of Faith

Take God's first step.

Many years ago, my son sent me a quote that I still have on my desk: "A man's shadow is larger the closer he is to the source." It seems like a simple concept, but to me it is profound. Even though many wise people have written scholarly texts on theology, and many eloquent speakers have presented inspiring sermons, all we really need for meaningful spiritual growth and to develop a steadfast faith-based life is to each day move one step closer towards God's light. It is within this light and in His presence that I hope you, too, will feel worthy and noble in His sight.

Acknowledgments

I would especially like to thank my husband for all his support and encouragement for completing this book.

I would like to sincerely thank all the family and friends with whom I have had the pleasure of afternoon tea.

Appreciation and thanks as well to:

Pamela Cangioli at Proofed to Perfection for her professional editing and encouragement.

Patricia Bacall Garver at Bacall Creative for her creativity and patience.

About the Author

Pamela Kennedy has embraced the opportunity of living in many regions of the United States. She enjoys both driving trips and visiting countries abroad. She especially values being termed a *traveler* rather than a *tourist*. She earned a Bachelor of Science in Computer Science from University of Florida. The desire to understand how different cultures connect with each other, especially through faith and religion, led her to later complete a Masters of Humanities from Sacramento State University. Appreciating unique moments from her family's tradition of afternoon tea inspired her to share these insights that she hopes will bring you encouragement and grow your faith. She currently lives with her husband and near family in Chesterfield, VA.

Made in the USA
Middletown, DE
12 January 2025